HAL•LEONARD
INSTRUMENTAL
PLAY-ALONG

CELLO

AUDIO ACCESS
INCLUDED

Piazzolla Tangos

T0081660

2 Ausencias (The Absent)
4 El viaje (The Voyage)
6 Chanson de la naissance (Song of the Birth)
8 Libertango
10 Los sueños (Dreams)
7 Milonga
12 Oblivion
13 Ouverture from *Famille d'artistes*
14 Sensuel (Sensual)
16 Sentimental
18 Sin rumbo (Aimless)
20 Street Tango
22 Tango final
17 Vuelvo al sur (I'm Returning South)

To access audio visit:
www.halleonard.com/mylibrary

Enter Code
4131-7047-7527-3330

ISBN 978-1-4950-2845-8

BOOSEY & HAWKES

AN IMAGEM COMPANY

DISTRIBUTED BY
HAL•LEONARD® CORPORATION
7777 W. BLUEMOUND RD. P.O. BOX 13819 MILWAUKEE, WI 53213

For all works contained herein:
Unauthorized copying, arranging, adapting, recording, Internet posting, public performance, or other distribution of the printed music in this publication is an infringement of copyright. Infringers are liable under the law.

www.boosey.com
www.halleonard.com

AUSENCIAS
(The Absent)

CELLO

ASTOR PIAZZOLLA

© Copyright by Lime Green Music Ltd.
This arrangement © 2015 by Lime Green Music Ltd.
Copyright for All Countries. All Rights Reserved.

rit.
a tempo
D.S. al Coda
CODA
rit.
p

EL VIAJE
(The Voyage)

CELLO

ASTOR PIAZZOLLA

© Copyright by Lime Green Music Ltd.
This arrangement © 2015 by Lime Green Music Ltd.
Copyright for All Countries. All Rights Reserved.

Slower
rit.

CHANSON DE LA NAISSANCE

(Song of the Birth)

from FAMILLE D'ARTISTES

CELLO

ASTOR PIAZZOLLA

© Copyright by Lime Green Music Ltd.
This arrangement © 2015 by Lime Green Music Ltd.
Copyright for All Countries. All Rights Reserved.

MILONGA

from A MIDSUMMER NIGHT'S DREAM

CELLO

ASTOR PIAZZOLLA

© Copyright by Lime Green Music Ltd.
This arrangement © 2015 by Lime Green Music Ltd.
Copyright for All Countries. All Rights Reserved.

LIBERTANGO

CELLO

ASTOR PIAZZOLLA

Copyright © 1975 Edizioni Curci S.r.l., Milan and A. Pagani S.r.l., Fino Mornasco (CO), Italy
Copyright Renewed
All Rights in the U.S. Controlled and Administered by Spirit Two Music, Inc. o/b/o Curci USA Music Publishing
All Rights in Canada Controlled and Administered by SMG Ash Music Canada o/b/o Curci USA Music Publishing
International Copyright Secured All Rights Reserved
This arrangement © 2015

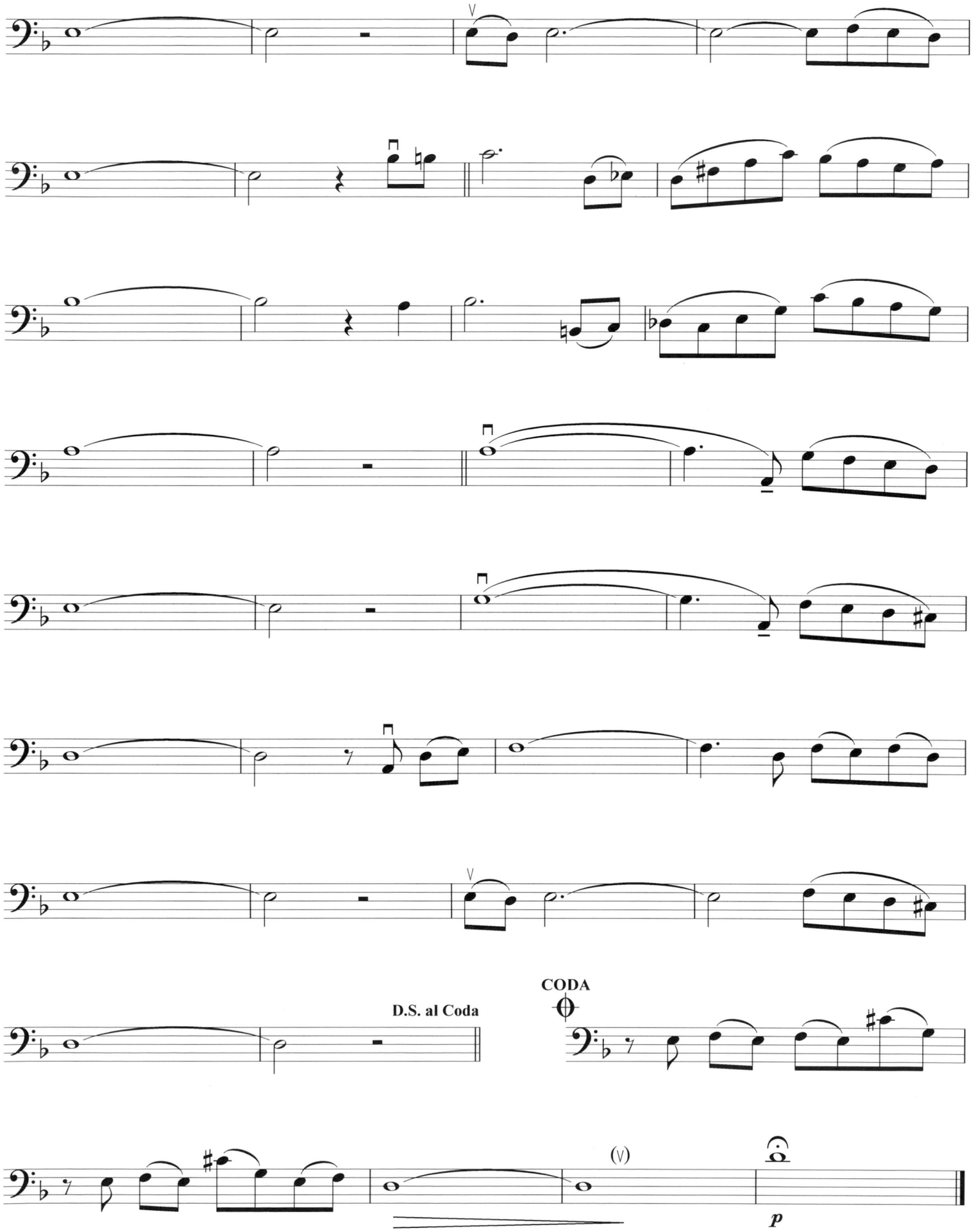
D.S. al Coda
CODA
p

LOS SUEÑOS

(Dreams)

from SUR

CELLO

ASTOR PIAZZOLLA

© Copyright by Lime Green Music Ltd.
This arrangement © 2015 by Lime Green Music Ltd.
Copyright for All Countries. All Rights Reserved.

mp
dim.
pp

OBLIVION

CELLO

ASTOR PIAZZOLLA

© 1984 by A. PAGANI S.r.l. Edizioni Musicali, Fino Mornasco (CO) Italy
This arrangement © 2015 by A. PAGANI S.r.l. Edizioni Musicali, Fino Mornasco (CO) Italy
Rights for USA Controlled by Stella Solaris Music
All Rights Reserved Used by Permission

OUVERTURE

from FAMILLE D'ARTISTES

CELLO

ASTOR PIAZZOLLA

© Copyright by Lime Green Music Ltd.
This arrangement © 2015 by Lime Green Music Ltd.
Copyright for All Countries. All Rights Reserved.

SENSUEL

(Sensual)

from A MIDSUMMER NIGHT'S DREAM

CELLO

ASTOR PIAZZOLLA

© Copyright by Lime Green Music Ltd.
This arrangement © 2015 by Lime Green Music Ltd.
Copyright for All Countries. All Rights Reserved.

2
mf
f
ff

SENTIMENTAL

from FAMILLE D'ARTISTES

CELLO

ASTOR PIAZZOLLA

© Copyright by Lime Green Music Ltd.
This arrangement © 2015 by Lime Green Music Ltd.
Copyright for All Countries. All Rights Reserved.

VUELVO AL SUR

(I'm Returning South)

CELLO

ASTOR PIAZZOLLA

© Copyright by Lime Green Music Ltd.
This arrangement © 2015 by Lime Green Music Ltd.
Copyright for All Countries. All Rights Reserved.

SIN RUMBO
(Aimless)

CELLO

ASTOR PIAZZOLLA

© Copyright by Lime Green Music Ltd.
This arrangement © 2015 by Lime Green Music Ltd.
Copyright for All Countries. All Rights Reserved.

rit.
a tempo
f
mp
rit.
p

STREET TANGO

CELLO

ASTOR PIAZZOLLA

© Copyright by Lime Green Music Ltd.
This arrangement © 2015 by Lime Green Music Ltd.
Copyright for All Countries. All Rights Reserved.

mp
accel.
f

TANGO FINAL

from FAMILLE D'ARTISTES

CELLO

ASTOR PIAZZOLLA

© Copyright by Lime Green Music Ltd.
This arrangement © 2015 by Lime Green Music Ltd.
Copyright for All Countries. All Rights Reserved.

mf
3
f
mf
rit.
Slower
3
rit.